EEO
AND THE
WHISTLEBLOWER

EEO AND THE WHISTLEBLOWER

Selfish Love and the Effect of Power

By Elisa Domingo Garcia

XULON PRESS ELITE

Xulon Press Elite
2301 Lucien Way #415
Maitland, FL 32751
407.339.4217
www.xulonpress.com

© 2021 by Elisa Domingo Garcia

Book cover done by Maresala Milo
milo92117@yahoo.com

All rights reserved solely by the author. The author guarantees all contents are original and do not infringe upon the legal rights of any other person or work. No part of this book may be reproduced in any form without the permission of the author. The views expressed in this book are not necessarily those of the publisher.

Due to the changing nature of the Internet, if there are any web addresses, links, or URLs included in this manuscript, these may have been altered and may no longer be accessible. The views and opinions shared in this book belong solely to the author and do not necessarily reflect those of the publisher. The publisher therefore disclaims responsibility for the views or opinions expressed within the work.

Printed in the United States of America.

Paperback ISBN-13: 978-1-6628-1667-3
Ebook ISBN-13: 978-1-6628-1668-0

Some names in this book have been changed to protect the innocent. This story takes place in one of the veterans hospitals. Its employees considered this place a paradise, with a bountiful, beautiful forest supplying them with delicious fruits, nutrients, and flowers that would sustain their happy and peaceful livelihood.

So, when evil men came to roost in this forest, the employees gave them appropriate names that describe their activities, calling them the snakes.

This book is not written to demean the Veterans Administration. The VA is an institution that honors and serves our veterans who sacrificed defending our country. Employees love and cherish each veteran and do their best to give well-deserved care to our beloved veterans. But like in any institution, a few bad apples can find a place in the VA.

Table of Contents

Dedication xi
Acknowledgements xiii
Introduction xv

Chapter 1	Author's Background. 1	
Chapter 2	The VA Pharmacy Atmosphere Under Pharmacy Director Ronald Dick 3	
Chapter 3	Love Beyond Reason 11	
Chapter 4	Happy Birthday, Queen Bee 17	
Chapter 5	How Paul Became a Whistleblower. 20	
Chapter 6	Beginning the Pursuit of Justice 23	
Chapter 7	Union President of Three States. 31	
Chapter 8	Suffering as a Victim 35	
Chapter 9	Cobra. 40	
Chapter 10	The Undesirables 43	
Chapter 11	The Victims. 46	
Chapter 12	Harassment. 52	
Chapter 13	The Violence. 58	
Chapter 14	A Patient Died 61	
Chapter 15	Applying for a Supervisor Job 63	
Chapter 16	The Helpers. 65	

Chapter 17	The Lawyer	68
Chapter 18	The Trial	69
Chapter 19	Result of the EEO	73
Chapter 20	Result on the Patient's Death	76
Chapter 21	Result of the Inspector General Investigation	78
Chapter 22	Being a Supervisor	80
Chapter 23	Tips on How to Get the Best Healthcare	82

Dedication

*A*gain, to the blessings of my life, my only children, LT. Col. Nelson of the US Army and Engineer Steve, who serves the US in another capacity.

To all our armed forces who guard our liberty.

To Ronald Dick, the pharmacy director, who loves our country, our military, and our veterans.

To Laurence Paul Pinheiro (known as Paul), the whistleblower, a hero, and an honorable Vietnam Veteran, who suffered atrocities in his effort in getting back stolen money from the VA.

Acknowledgements

JOAN JONES – a veteran, a very intelligent, caring black lady, with a Pharm D Pharmacy degree, a friend who helped, encouraged, and gave me inspiration to write this book.

Introduction

I am a pharmacist, and one day, I came home from work perplexed. I had just received another write-up, me second write-up in one week. Again and again, I asked myself, "Why?" I had worked in this hospital for more than eight years now, and nobody had complained about me. I always worked hard to the best of my ability, for I love this country and the veterans we serve. What is happening? My father often told us, his children, "When something worries you, turn to God." At that moment, I looked around and saw the Bible.

I picked it up to console myself. Opening it, lo and behold, I was on the Psalms, Psalm 35 in particular: "Prayers for Help against Unjust Enemies." I read it, and it says,

> *Fight Oh Lord Against Those Who Fight Me, War against Those who make war upon me, Take Up the shield and buckler, and rise up in my defense. Brandish the lance and block the way. In the face of my pursuers, say to my soul, "I am your salvation. Let those be put to shame and disgraced, who seek my life, be turned back and confounded, who plot*

> *evil against me. Let them be like chaff before the wind, with the angel of the Lord driving them on, let their way be dark and slippery, with the angel of the Lord pursuing them.*

I continued praying "The Holy Spirit Counsel":

> *Feel secure even in trials, knowing that trials produce patience, from patience comes merit, merit is the source of hope, and hope does not disappoint us because the Holy Spirit has been given to us, pouring into our hearts the love of God.*

I felt relief and worry leave me. Each day, I prayed, for I knew the Lord was with me and would protect me.

EEO (EQUAL EMPLOYMENT OPPORTUNITY)

EEO, or Equal Employment Opportunity, is used as an instrument for an employee victim, giving the victim rights to be upheld in a process presided by a federal judge. Very rarely does someone who applies for EEO win their cases, for obvious reasons. The cause of an EEO application is mostly an atrocity that management has done to the employee. Witnesses are afraid to talk, about EEO cases that are under investigation for they might also become victims, or most of all, they are afraid of losing their jobs, for many have families to feed. An employer, a supervisor, or anyone in a higher office position has power over an employee. They frame, harass, discriminate, and even do bodily harm to disgruntled employees to get rid of them. Their helpers are unscrupulous people who desire higher wages and accessibility for higher positions. They even cooperate, manipulate, change, or erase records that the whistleblowers and friends of the whistleblowers have established. They become false witnesses, doing whatever they were told to harass the victim. They destroy the purpose of EEO, not allowing justice to be given to the person who applied for it.

WHISTLEBLOWERS

Whistleblowers bring to light the worst people who have the power in an establishment, which is why they are usually in danger, both physically and mentally. Whistleblowers have been fired from their jobs, humiliated, and disgraced for telling the truth, because they stood up for what is right. There were many veterans who then worked with the Veterans Hospitals who became whistleblowers. Even their loved ones suffered from the atrocities inflicted upon them when people acquired power within these august institutions and harmed their physiological and psychological wellbeing.

The health of whistleblowers often deteriorates due to internal harassment by mean and powerful supervisors. After being humiliated, supervisors often change their job for a harder one, lose their jobs, or are even escorted out by the VA police where they work. Many employees witness this, yet they keep quiet for fear of becoming victims themselves. At the VA hospital, several whistleblowers died in disgraced. They guarded the VA property and reported lots of misconduct to the Inspector General. Most of the time, the result is that the VA gets back funds that have been stolen and the guilty are imprisoned.

PHARMACY STAFF

1. RONALD DICK – The very best Pharmacy Director. He is very intelligent and respected, and he mentors many. He is fair in his dealings with employees under him and loved by the staff under him.

2. LAURENCE PAUL PINHEIRO (well known as Paul) – The whistleblower, and a Vietnam veteran who loves this country and became a victim.

3. KING SHORTY – The Pharmacy Terror, also secretly named "the Big Viper." He is the acting pharmacy director.

4. COBRA – Secretly named after the snake that danced from his country of origin. He is the inpatient pharmacy supervisor.

5. THE RATTLE SNAKE – Secretly called "The Rattle Snake," he is a pharmacy technician who became a traitor to the person who treated him as her own son.

6. WISE TURTLE – The former pharmacy technician who became the union president of three states, California, Nevada, and Arizona.

7. THE UNDESIRABLES – These are senior employees who are also whistleblowers, as well as their friends and those who opposed King Shorty's management.

Chapter 1
Author's Background

Every day before I left my car to go to work, I would pray, "Lord, be with me. Help me give the best care to my patients. Give me understanding, intelligence, and love in caring for them. Be my guide and don't let me make mistakes."

I studied pharmacy in the most prestigious and expensive university in the Far East, Santo Tomas University, built in the year 1521. I received a bachelor's degree in pharmacy. Many foreign students from around the world also come to study there, and they win scholarships and earn degrees from this university. I then immigrated to the Unites States and worked with the Veterans Hospital, first as a pharmacy technician in an unbiased setting, since I didn't yet have my pharmacy license in the States at the time. At night, I would study at USC for a postgraduate degree in pharmacy. Finally, I received my license as a registered pharmacist in Nevada.

I applied as a registered pharmacist at the Veterans Hospital and was accepted. I noticed the beauty of the environment where I would be working. The Lord is really good to me. I stopped to give God a little prayer of thanks.

Mr. Ronald Dick, the Pharmacy Director, is the best pharmacy director I have ever encountered in my **twenty-three years** of service with the Veterans Hospital. After retirement, I worked **another ten years** as an "on-call pharmacist" in different VA Hospitals and Native American Indian Hospitals. All in all for a total of thirty three years, I practiced Pharmacy. In this capacity, I became subordinate to every pharmacy director in every hospital I worked for. Still, I consider Mr. Ronald Dick the best pharmacy director I have ever encountered in my total thirty-three years of pharmacy practice.

Chapter 2

The VA Pharmacy Atmosphere Under Pharmacy Director Ronald Dick

Most of the time, the inpatient pharmacy was a very happy place to work, even if it was usually busy. There was camaraderie, cooperation, and respect shared between all the pharmacy technicians, interns, and supply staff; everyone was mostly efficient and followed all procedures. The pharmacists did the same, so all in all, the environment was a very pleasant place to work. Mr. Ronald Dick, the pharmacy director, was a very considerate boss, and he cared for his employees and was very congenial to his subordinates. He motivated and encouraged people under him without being pushy. He was a mentor to many and gave responsibility to very efficient employees; thus, there were big possibilities for advancement for the staff. Mr. Dick looked at his employee as individuals and said that every person had something positive to offer. He was one of the smartest, humblest, kindest, most decent men, and he inspired people to work with dignity and appreciation. He was a man with good morals, and he listened and responded to others with clarity under pressure, while embodying great compassion for people experiencing difficulty in their lives. He recognized talents and reciprocated good ideas from subordinates. He was fair in his dealings with those working under him.

Working at this hospital, I interacted with colleagues, professionals in diverse health care fields, subordinates, and patients. I socialized outside of the VA, as well attended different organizations, even becoming president of one named FACES. This organization encouraged high school students to study hard, and those who did were given monetary awards to help in their pursuits of college education. I celebrated with my colleagues on different occasions, and most important to me, the people with whom I associated showed integrity, good morals, and a deep love for this country—veterans in particular.

The hospital where I worked was near a medical university. Almost all medical and pharmacy students from this university and pharmacy students from different universities around the country did their internships with us, as well as with hospitals on the locality to widen their expertise. We, the pharmacist staff, were their mentors. My colleagues and I used our professional attributes to serve our veterans to the best of our ability. I say this because I love this country and my only children chose to serve this country as a soldier and in another capacity. Many of my colleagues and other health care professionals were veterans themselves. We were very much aware of the sacrifices the veterans incurred and made, their injuries, the deaths of their buddies in the field of combat, and how families and loved ones have coped during their distressful tours of duty.

There were many activities in the VA, and many times, I was one of the leaders. There was Diversity Day, where all ethnic groups showed their special talents in the program. It is amazing how countries differ in their dances, yet each one has its beauty to behold—the movement of the hands and feet and the expressions of smiles and happy faces differ with each dance, but each has its own allure. Their different attires representing their own countries seem to made by distinguished designers; each had its own colors in gold, red, blue, or silver, shimmering in every movement made. Almost everyone wore the special clothing of their country of origin. Some employees did the American Square Dance, and Indian girls from India performed a dance while asking a man to marry them. That was one of the interpretations we were told while the dance was on display. The bamboo dance from the Philippines which Philippine nurses performed received much applause. The intricate steps of Irish dancers made the audience clap their hands and sway back and forth; it was wonderful to watch. The colorful gowns of the Mexicans got lots of "Wows" from the audience. Italians, Germans, and others from several countries exhibited their unique apparels with their extraordinary dances. In one section of the compounds were small stalls, erected for the occasion, where countries displayed their main products; all were very interesting. Each stall had a small flag of its country on the top. Everyone can learn much about the countries' cultures and what is best in their economies. Overall, there was unity, respect, and understanding of each one's culture, and friendship and camaraderie developed.

There was also a show in karate, which was very funny yet effective in self-defense. During the show, this very old man was walking down the street, and two hoodlums decided to rob him. They approached him and said, "Give us your wallet!" The old man raised his cane simultaneously inverting the cane's hook's handle and caught one of the hoodlum's neck. He pulled it, and the guy fell on his face. At the same time, he instantly kicked the other hoodlum in the groin. The man started hoping around, holding his groin. The audience began applauding and hollering with laughter. The old man gave many more defensive antics, and the audience cheered and gave a standing ovation. Additionally, Martin Luther King Jr. Day was celebrated with much fanfare. On all occasions, food was plenty, and employees and veterans all had a really wonderful day.

The Veteran's Hospital where I worked had a wonderful outdoor environment. In the lush, green campus, a manmade lake surrounded the main building and the nursing homes. On breaks, employees usually took a walk in this peaceful, beautiful environment, where they could relax their minds and bodies or enjoy companionship with friends who worked in the same place. During winter months, migrating birds usually dropped by, and duck populations would swim with their young ones in tow. Sometimes birds of different kinds frolicked in the lake. I spotted some marshes where the ducks had laid their eggs. One time, the eggs had disappeared, and I wondered if a hungry veteran or his family had taken the eggs. How pitiful that should be, for lots of our veterans were poor and had a hard time looking for jobs.

Sometimes funny things happened with the ducks. Many times, doctors would bring bread in paper bags to feed them. Some ducks would even try to take a bite of the paper bags that had the bread in them. The ducks would keep on following the doctors, making quacking sounds: "Quack, quack, quack, quack!" The sound they made was so loud. Everybody would laugh, for it seemed the ducks were saying that the doctors were "quack" doctors. The doctors didn't mind the laughter, and they themselves even laughed as they continued feeding the ducks. They loved to feed the ducks, for often some mother ducks had some chicks either swimming or on land with them. The sight was so loving and caring, and many employees would come to watch.

While working or in other places of the building, we were often interrupted by the intercom, which would state in a booming voice, "CODE BLUE, CODE BLUE," and then it would mention a specific place. I attended countless code blues. My heart would beat faster as I listened intently to find out the location of the code. One pharmacy technician would be bringing the pharmacy cart loaded with necessary medications. Locations could be anywhere—on stairs, in bathrooms, in the canteen, outside the buildings, and even in the chapel. I would run as fast as I could, for I knew that a veteran's life was at stake. To me, a soldier's life is very precious, for I have seen the sacrifices, the dedication, the humiliation, and the love that these soldiers have for our country. I remember the joys every time the code blue team was able to save a life, as well as the sadness and disappointment when we did not succeed.

THE NORTHRIDGE EARTHQUAKE

When all department employees worked side by side the whole night and several days after the Northridge earthquake, everyone shared camaraderie. Patients that could not be accommodated in another VA hospital began arriving at two o'clock in the morning. The moment a patient stepped down from the bus or was brought down in a stretcher, his name tag was placed around his wrist. The doctor then interviewed and checked the patient. While walking toward the building to house the patient, the doctor barked orders to the nurse and pharmacist. By the time the patient reached his designated room, his bed was ready, his medications were ready to take, and the nurse was already monitoring his vitals, if there was a need for it. What teamwork! What an accomplishment! Afterward, we were very tired but very happy, for we had been able to render an extraordinary job to the benefit of our beloved veterans.

All departments had the same goal: to achieve the most prestigious award for organized performance excellence in the Department of Veterans Affairs, The Robert W. Carey Performance Excellence Award. This award was based on the Malcolm Baldrige criteria for performance excellence. We earned this award for the year 2003. Oh, what an accomplishment! Oh, what dedications! Oh, what joy we felt that our hospital was the best in the whole nation! Those were moments to cherish forever! The hospital received a monetary award, so everyone got a stipend.

One of my dreams is to see to it that *no* veteran is begging or sleeping on side roads or looking for food in trash bins, and that all of them without exception are well taken care of, together with their families. After seeing only a small glimpse of their sacrifices, like toddlers running after their father or mother before being deployed or seeing them training covered with sweat and nearly collapsed due to exhaustion, I wonder why many do not appreciate them.

One experience that is forever etched in my mind was when I visited my son at Desert Palm Springs. There was a sandstorm, so my husband and I sought shelter in a building. We were looking through a glass window and saw two individuals who looked like zombies coming toward the building where we were. The two figures were all white, covered with sand, and their green uniforms had become snow white. One of them was my son, and both figures were covered with sand, with lots going in their ears, nose, and eyes due to the strong wind. All around were tents where the soldiers would sleep, and sand was covering the top of all of the tents.

I told my son, "I'll get you a hotel."

With a crisp voice, he answered, "How about my people?" He was a captain at the time. "Mom, I am one of them. We have to learn how to be tough and be able to cope with whatever comes our way."

Seeing the wounded, the hurt, or the expressions on the faces of loved ones lost is unforgettable. This moment made me wish that all soldiers who served would get an increase in their benefits, be given the opportunity for jobs, and receive the best health care the world can provide. It is unbelievable that our soldiers' pay is so low. As some people say, they meet bullets in their work, while many received millions catching a ball. Many Americans do not even appreciate the freedom they have due to the efforts of our soldiers. This freedom is maintained only because of the love and efforts of our soldiers who love this country more than life itself.

I hope the American people will open their eyes and no longer take it for granted that our soldiers are in the same category of citizens who work and enjoy the benefit of a happy, free living. Our soldiers are different from citizens. Many times, they are separated from their love ones. They have missed seeing their children grow up, the joy their children experience in sports and in school, and even the pain when their children cry. Many consider them soldiers and think that they don't have ambition. The truth is that our soldiers love this country most of all, so they are ready to sacrifice, even to die, for this unwavering love. This love exhibits intelligence, strength of character, dedication, and firm purpose to accomplish the best in their goals.

Chapter 3

Love Beyond Reason

When Ronald Dick, the pharmacy director, retired, the pharmacy staff realized how good he was and missed him, especially when the assistant pharmacy director, King Shorty, temporarily came into power until a new director was hired. He stated that he was now the king and had new plans for the pharmacy staff to follow. He firmly said that he would be promoted to the position of the new director. King Shorty was short in stature as well as short in morals, which many in the pharmacy staff believed after he became the acting pharmacy director. Under his management, the pharmacy environment drastically changed. King Shorty was also secretly called the Big Viper.

THE COMING OF QUEEN BEE

Oh love, what can it do? As Shakespeare says in *The Merchant of Venice,* "Love is blind and lovers cannot see the pretty follies, they themselves commit." How true this was for that is what happened in the VA Hospital, where I worked for more than eight years.

One Saturday around nine o'clock in the morning, I was the only pharmacist in the VA. The hospital housed three hundred beds at that time, excluding the nursing homes, of which I was also in charge. I don't know how many patients we had then, but it was very busy. The outpatient pharmacy was closed, as it was a weekend, and I was working on the second floor, in the inpatient pharmacy as the pharmacist in charge. The pharmacist on duty was also in charge of the security of the outpatient and inpatient pharmacies during holidays, nights, and weekends. Often on weekends, the pharmacist would go down to the outpatient pharmacy to get narcotics from the pharmacy vault.

On this day, we did not have enough narcotics available in the inpatient pharmacy, so I went down to the outpatient pharmacy to get some narcotics to replenish our supply. To go to the outpatient pharmacy, one had to pass through the door where the offices of the pharmacy director and his assistant director were located. On opening the door, I was shocked to see a woman sitting on one of the chairs outside of the offices. I was not aware that anyone including the acting pharmacy director and his guest were there. At that time, no one was supposed to enter the pharmacy without my knowledge since I was in charge and accountable for the security of the drugs. I blurted out, "Who are you, and what are you doing here?"

She said, "Oh, I am meeting with Mr. Shorty, acting pharmacy director, and I am applying for a job as a pharmacist."

"Where is he?" I asked her.

She said, "He just went out to get some papers."

"Oh, I see," I said. "I will leave you here since you said he will be back."

I took the necessary narcotics and went back to the second floor, for it was very busy and a code blue might be called. In the meantime, I was thinking, *Why on weekends, when human resources is closed?* Also, I doubted the legality of it. Since I was busy working as the only pharmacist on duty, I completely forgot the incident and told no one about it.

After several days, I was happy because we had more help, for the woman was hired and started working with us. The new employee was a pretty married woman, just like Mr. Shorty, the acting pharmacy director, who was also married, but *not* to each other. I am not one to indulge in gossip or watch co-workers in their personal activities. For this reason, I was not aware that this woman in the pharmacy was secretly named "the Chosen One" or "the Queen Bee." Every time the Chosen One came into the pharmacy, someone always greet her with "Hi, Mrs. Shorty." She would just smile and go on her way. I was puzzled, for I knew her last name to be different, and both she and Mr. Shorty were married to other people. So, I thought the staff was just teasing her.

I believed that everyone presumed that Mr. Shorty was in love with the Chosen One, which is why they also referred to her as the Queen Bee—because of their behavior and his preferential treatment of her. One time, there was a movie presentation in the pharmacy, and Mr. Shorty was standing behind the Chosen One's chair while watching the presentation. Everybody was quiet and not looking at the movie, for their attention was focused on those two people. Many incidents occurred in which the Chosen One and Mr. Shorty were close together, such as while waiting for the elevator, during official meetings, at pharmacy parties, and during office hours. There was nothing like touching or kissing, yet when together, the atmosphere seemed electrically charged and the staff almost always focused their attention on the two of them. At any occasion, there was always silence when they were present, and people around just kept on watching them. The attraction was so obvious that most of the staff called the Chosen One "Mrs. Shorty," both behind her back and even to her face, laughing afterwards. The Chosen One never corrected the name, and she seemed happy to be called "Mrs. Shorty."

Later, many members of the staff came to believe that the Queen Bee wanted pharmacist vacancies in the VA. She had just come from another country where English was not taught in their schools. Many of her co-pharmacists had immigrated to the US, and they had to take the Pharmacist Board Examination to get a license. It was amazing how many received pharmacist licenses when they didn't speak English fluently, especially because the examination even had essays. It was rumored that one of the state board pharmacist members came from this same country, so many passed the examination, even though they didn't speak English fluently and were short in their vocabulary. Many were seeking jobs, and it would be easy for them to acquire the position of a pharmacist in the VA, since the Queen Bee had Mr. Shorty to back them up. Many of them were having a hard time seeking jobs due to their inefficiency in the English language and their diction.

Pharmacists had to counsel patients concerning their medications, and many veterans complained because they couldn't understand them. They opted to mail their medications rather than wait for three to four hours to be counseled in pidgin English.

Within two months, the Queen Bee's **two children** were also hired as pharmacists in the outpatient pharmacy. Many members of the pharmacy staff stated that the Chosen One's influence and preferential position enabled her **two children** to be hired in the same department. Is this not against federal law as a conflict of interest? Having the Chosen One for a mother enabled these individuals to get jobs in the VA system. Later, one of them was told to quit for an obvious reason: Mr. Shorty's action of hiring them was against the law.

When Mr. Shorty became the acting pharmacy director, people became suspicious that they were being spied upon and were afraid of losing their job. It was well known that the acting pharmacy director had intentions of hiring young people, and he issued a statement saying, "I will inject new blood in the pharmacy staff. I will change the atmosphere of the pharmacy staff." The staff came to believe that Mr. Shorty considered himself a king and that he would change the staff to younger people, disregarding the services of many who had already worked there for several years. The middle-aged and senior employees, who had been working happily for many, many years in this facility, were now worried that they might lose their jobs. If they resigned or sought other employment, they would lose their pensions. They worked quietly and seemed to be waiting for the ax to fall. The relaxed atmosphere was gone, and the staff became uptight and nervous while working.

King Shorty deliberately changed the diverse composition of the pharmacy staff; however, his relationship with the new female pharmacist came to light. Based on a picture taken in 2003 for Pharmacy Team of the Month, **50 percent** of the **pharmacist staff** were the **same ethnic group.** I still have a copy of the picture. One can deduct that the acting pharmacy director favored this ethnic group, to which the supposed loved one, the Queen

Bee, belonged. The normal channel for hiring staff was no longer followed. Interviews showed that the acting pharmacy director himself was prejudiced in his decisions to change the composition of the pharmacy staff. In his own words, he **repeatedly** stated his preference. As mentioned before, he had said, "I will inject new blood in the pharmacy staff." For instance, an experienced **black PhD in Pharmacy,** who was also a **veteran**, was denied employment when she applied to the VA hospital for the position of outpatient pharmacy supervisor. She had been a former pharmacist in the same VA for two years, had excellent work records, and decided to come back. A **newly graduated PhD in pharmacy** who was in the **same ethnic group as Queen Bee** was accepted for the position, and she was **not** a veteran. She did not even have the experience to be a supervisor. Meanwhile, the background and experience of the black PhD Pharmacist exceeded the criteria for qualification as outpatient pharmacy supervisor. This was a cut-case of discrimination.

Also, one black pharmacy technician was a true model of service. Everybody at the VA called him "Saint Thom" for his dedication to duty, his integrity, and his patience with being push around. The staff often said, "Do this," and "Do that," but he never complained. He did his best to accommodate everyone's wishes. His dedication to duty was exemplary, but when evaluated, he always received an average grade while others in his category who had performed with substandard level received outstanding grades. As the saying goes, "You must be twice as good to be considered good," and the "Saint" exceeded in his performance.

Chapter 4
Happy Birthday, Queen Bee

One day in June, a big sign was posted in both the inpatient and outpatient pharmacies. The sign stated that everybody was invited to Queen Bee's birthday party, which was to be held the next day in a newly created pharmacy breakroom. In whispers, everyone was asking who was attending, but it seemed that nobody was interested. However, some of the staff said, "We will all go so we won't miss the show," and everybody then agreed.

The next day around ten o'clock in the morning, Queen Bee's ethnic friends arrived with lots of food and began decorating the breakroom. They scattered balloons around the room. Many attended the party, but Queen Bee's friends were the only ones who brought food, drinks, and gifts. The staff present started eating, alternating with the others on duty so that everybody could come and enjoy the feast. The food was good, with lots of variety: spaghetti, chicken, sandwiches, salads, tacos, soups, and even cookies. A variety of soft drinks were on one table, and a big decorated cake was ushered in on a table with wheels. Fifteen minutes before eleven o'clock, Queen Bee, King Shorty, and Cobra, secretly named by the Pharmacy staff, the Inpatient Pharmacy Supervisor, arrived, and lively music began to play. There was a knock on the door, and a teenaged delivery boy entered with a bouquet of red roses. The card attached to the roses read, "Happy Birthday, Queen Bee, from King Shorty." After delivering the flowers, the delivery boy disappeared.

Queen Bee's face lit up with happiness. She kept on saying to King Shorty, "Oh, my favorite, red roses! Thank you, thank you!" all the while smelling the roses.

Suddenly, she let out a piercing scream. "Eeek, eeek, eeek, eeek, eeek!" She threw the flowers on the floor. Crawling on one of her hands was a huge cockroach, and another one crept around on the floor among the flowers that she had thrown down. Almost everyone turned to the counter where the platters of food were located. Their shoulders shook as they hid their laughter.

"Catch that delivery boy!" King Shorty shouted. Queen Bee's friends rushed out searching for the boy, but nobody found him. King Shorty called the flower shop, but it was the wrong number and there was no flower shop with that name around that vicinity. King Shorty's face was livid with anger. "The one who did this will be fired," he said.

One by one, the undesirable staff went out, throwing their unfinished food into the garbage can. I heard one employee say, "Nobody messed up with seasoned soldiers." They say that even the FBI could not locate the source of the flowers. It was rumored the teenaged delivery boy went one floor up, went to one bathroom, removed his wig, change his clothes, and went out with a backpack. Another older man came out from the bathroom with him, discussing about a patient, and together, they rode the elevator down and exited the building. All the undesirable party guest who worked in the inpatient pharmacy were now gathered there, happily looking at one another. Some were whispering with lots of giggles and laughter. What a blissful day everyone had!

Chapter 5
How Paul Became a Whistleblower

The outpatient pharmacy was swamped with many unfilled prescriptions, as several patients would leave instead of waiting for their prescriptions to be filled. Many patients stated that they couldn't understand the pharmacist who counseled them, and the pharmacists counseling them told them they were rude for they continuing to ask for repetition on what the pharmacists were saying. The pharmacists' diction was so terrible that everyone had a hard time understanding them, so the patients preferred their medications to be mailed.

We, the inpatient pharmacy staff, were told to work overtime to help process the overload prescriptions in outpatient pharmacy. I came in at four o'clock in the morning. One pharmacy technician who was also a member of the union was already there. The staff called him "Wise Turtle," for he knew how to avoid work and was very slow in accomplishing his assignments. He was not well liked by the pharmacy staff, as he spent most of his time in the office of the union president, who was a friend of his and also in his same ethnic group. Other technicians even did his work, and management remained quiet about it all.

"Good morning," I said to him. He nodded and went to the mailing bin, where boxes of drugs were to be mailed. He dropped a big box into the bin. I went to the files of prescriptions to be checked by a pharmacist. In came Laurence Paul, Pinheiro, commonly known as Paul, a Pharmacy Technician, and a veteran. He asked me, "What is the lazy bum doing here?" pointing to the technician in the process of again dumping a big bag of drugs in the mailing bin.

"Oh, please, Paul," I said, "Be nice. He is helping."

When Wise Turtle saw Paul, he said, "I am going to Inpatient Pharmacy upstairs, for I have duties to do there."

"Go ahead," I answered, and he left.

Paul went to the mailing bin, picked up the big bag, and asked me, "Is not our territory from Barstow to San Diego only?"

I responded, "I believe so."

"Why is this drug going to New York?" he asked.

I answered, "Maybe New York needs some drugs and is borrowing from us."

"Why don't they go to their supplier?"

"I don't know," I said, "and I am very busy, so don't bother me, for these prescriptions are already late and patients need them."

Paul then went to the telephone to call somebody. Then he started to work hard, as usual. My main concern was my job, and the patients waiting for their prescriptions. I later found out that Paul was calling the **Inspector General.** Paul asked the IG to investigate why drugs in our facility were being mailed to New York when our territory was only from Barstow to San Diego. In this case, Wise Turtle was not wise, for he had even used the VA registry to record the drugs he was mailing.

Paul was a happy veteran. He was very responsible, and his personality depicted that of a soldier most of the time. He would tell lots of jokes to his co-workers using military slang, as when a soldier is in a battle. I understood the jokes, for I had been around many military families and attended parties for my son, who is now a high-ranking officer in the army. Those who were not in the military were not used to such language and were baffled; several times, they would ask him the meaning of what he had said. After his explanations, we all laughed, and he would say, "Oh, you poor, innocent babes."

One of the jokes was so funny that I still laugh remembering it. He said that he would test our intelligence to see who the smartest was. He then began telling a story. "Two soldiers, one the captain and the other his aid, woke up in the middle of the night. Looking up were millions of beautiful, twinkling stars and the bright moon. The captain said to his aid, 'How wonderful God is to create such beauty.' He mentioned many things about the constellations, how some stars were named for different gods and others were named for new births. Then he asked the aid, 'What do you think?'"

Paul asked us the same question. "What do you think?" We all gave different answers. He said, "It seems nobody is smart in this group," and started laughing. Paul went on to say that the aid answered the captain, "Sir, I think somebody stole our tent." We all laughed, and that is why many wanted to work with Paul. His jokes were endless when there were breaks in the pharmacy. Often, he would say, "I think I am the most dumb one, for I could not help loving you all dumb ones." Then he would howl with laughter.

Chapter 6
Beginning the Pursuit of Justice

It became apparent that Paul had initiated an investigation by the IG. The torture then started by weekly write-ups. The complaints came from people who were jealous of Paul, such as those who hated his tough stand on working hard, as many would fool around during office hours. There were also the obvious reasons that many were brownnosing to the pharmacy supervisor and the acting pharmacy director. For more than three years, Paul was continually harassed. He received countless false reports and write-ups done by evil supporters of management. These people were mean and without human compassion, especially the Queen Bee. Her influence was so huge that work assigned to her was light and many helped her. The usual input on doctors' orders that pharmacists would make was three hundred or more prescriptions a day. Queen Bee only input below ten prescriptions a day, averaging seven prescriptions a day, of which I had still copies. Many believed she had a heart of stone, for several who worked with her suffered in various ways. Queen Bee had many people written up for reasons they were not even aware of. Those who helped her simply desired a raise in their salary or higher positions in their jobs.

These people wanted Paul to be fired because the investigation was in progress. Several times, the VA police escorted him out of the facility when he came to work. Also, when he became extremely sick and was seeking treatment, his prescriptions were not filled. He was entitled to be treated, since he was a veteran. Many witnesses were astounded at why this was happening, but they were scared to be witnesses because they could lose their job.

SUSPENSION PROPOSALS FOR LAURENCE PAUL PINHEIRO

TO: Mr. ████████

FROM: Mr. Lawrence Paul PINHEIRO

SUBJECT: Suspension Proposal

DATE: January 4, 1996

    I am appalled at the resurrection of such flagrant charges that are based on false statements, statements taken out of the context, and absolute false charges.

    To Charge One, where is there substantiating proof such as statements, witnesses or other proof that such a statement was made by me or anyone else ?

    To the second charge, which is given as a direct quote from me, I am alleged to have referred to my supervisor as a male Filipino. There is no male Filipino employed in the Pharmacy and it is absolute nonsense that I would make such a statement. That Mr. ████████████ quotes me directly as referring to my supervisor on this date of Thanksgiving 1994 as a male Filipino while all supervisors that day were ladies as evidence of Mr. Harrise's sexist thinking. While such thinking is unforgivable in any employee, in so-called management personnel it is unpardonable.

    You stated in a conversation with me on 15 Dec. 1994 that it was not your wish to re-start suspension against me, and were forced to by the Union, ████████ and ████████, and HRMS employee ████████. This I wish to persue at the highest levels of appeal and / or the Federal Court System. It is well known that the union / management partnership has been bastardized in this instance. I shall present incontrovertible proof at the proper forum.

    While you make pretenses at the dignity of the V.A. Pharmacy as a workplace, you failed to take any action whatever when you were given notice, in front of a witness, that a Registry employee working in the V.A. Pharmacy was stalking and terrorizing a student throughout the V.A., the pharmacy, and V.A. grounds. As witnesses to this I will present, during my appeal, statements from four F.T.E.'s of the V.A. Pharmacy. I cite this as proof of ongoing harassment and hostility to me. Article 10 - Section 1 (A).

Article 10 - Section 1 (A3)
    At the Pharmacy Staff Meeting of December 20, 1995, you threatened mass retaliation, during the meeting. Signed statements and oral evidence will be given at the proper forum(s).

Article 10 - Section 4
During the Board of Investigation, January - February 1995, my rights were repetedly violated. All "evidence" from this board is thus tainted.

Article 10 - Section 5
Your own statement that you did not wish to see this suspension re-started, but were under orders from Personnel and the Union and even intimating ▓▓▓▓ of the E.E.O., cause me to assert that the I.G. Investigation which is forthcoming is the sole cause for the re-starting of this ill-conceived suspension.

Article 10 - Section 8
The date of the re-surfacing of this suspension and the statements of ▓▓▓▓▓▓▓▓ give tremendous evidentiary fact that my rights have again been violated.

Article 10 - Section 8
In that there was an ongoing problem in September, October and November of 1994 with my being locked out of the Pharmacy and while never being shown ▓▓▓▓▓▓▓▓▓▓▓▓▓▓' Report of Contact, I was assured by ▓▓▓▓▓▓▓▓▓▓ that management's failure to assure me access to my work area had been corrected and this would also resolve ▓▓▓▓▓▓▓' report of contact and thus resolve the problem at the lowest possible level. This now appears to be another lie by pharmacy management. By being reprisal against me, both Article 10 Section 8 and Article 13 Section 6 are violated.

Article 11 - Section 4 (c)
That I was not actually shown a Report of Contact from ▓▓▓▓▓▓▓▓▓▓ until 7 months after it was written.

Article 12 - Section 3
By not having given me a formal reprimand and skipping from informal counseling to suspension, my rights are again violated.

Article 12 - Section 5
I was repeatedly denied Union representation during the so-called Board of Investigation of January-February 1995.
This violated again my rights.

Article 12 - Section 6 (c)
I was not apprised fully of my rights by this so-called Board of Investigation. It was a kangaroo court and properly signed statements by those called for statements will be given at the proper forum during my appeal. My rights again were repeatedly violated.

Article 12 - Section 6 (D)
My rights were violated totally by this:
▬▬▬▬▬▬▬ - Union representative ▬▬▬▬.
Signed statements will be given as proof at the proper forum.

Article 12 - Section 7 (A)
No 30 day notice given - again violating my rights.

Article 12 - Section 7 (A)
I requested, in writing to ▬▬▬▬▬▬, one copy of any document(s) in the evidence file be provided to me and was refused, in writing. This was against my Guaranteed Rights.

Article 12 - Section 9
When I met with ▬▬▬▬▬▬, AFGE officer, I was informed that the V.A. never informed him of the decision to suspend me. This is yet another violation.

Article 13 - Section 6
There has not been any attempt whatsoever to informally resolve this. My rights have not been protected.

Article 13 - Section 7
I have attempted to talk with ▬▬▬▬▬▬, repeatedly.
I have attempted to talk with ▬▬▬▬, EEO, repeatedly.
I have attempted to speak with ▬▬▬▬▬▬, repeatedly.
I have attempted to talk with other EEO counselors, Union officials, ▬▬▬▬ and ▬▬▬▬
In all instances I have been refused an audience or had reprisal taken against me by my supervisor.
As I have repeatedly asked, both at the V.A. for three years, and of ▬▬▬▬▬, Congressman, who has documented my case for one year:
Why are my rights so repeatedly stomped on?

Article 13 - Section 9
My first written complaints - dated January/February of 1995 - have yet to even be addressed. This violates my rights.

Article 13 - Section 10
I do not, at this time, consent to combining my multiple complaints, past and present.

Article 14 - Section 3
I do not, at this time, consent to expediting my past complaints, as recorded in the files of Congressman ▬▬▬▬▬.

Article 24 - Section 9
   Stress and hostility affect health. I have spoken with ▓▓▓▓ for two years about the gradual development of problems in the Pharmacy. Again I suffer reprisal from management. This will be addressed at the proper forum.

Article 28 - Section 5 (B)
   Despite requests repeatedly made to ▓▓▓▓▓▓▓▓ and ▓▓▓▓, I have been refused my rights. Date stamped evidence from January/February 1995 will be presented at the proper forum.

Article 28 - Section 7 (B)
   I have never even been able to get my rights explained to me. This is against my Guaranteed Rights and witnesses will be presented at the proper forum.

   After all is said and done, I assert there to be an ongoing conspiracy to run me off my job and I will present further evidence at the proper forum.

   All threats of suspension should be lifted until the hostile environment that exists in the Pharmacy has been fully investigated along with multiple allegations concerning repeatedly depriving me of my rights.

                    Respectfully,

                    Lawrence Paul PINHEIRO
                    Pharmacy Technician

CC - Files
     Congressman ▓▓▓▓▓
     Office of I.G.
     San Francisco Reg. E.E.O.
     Mr. ▓▓▓▓▓
     President ▓▓▓▓▓
     V.F.W.
     V.V.A.
     D.A.V.
     American Legion

I had to retire for both my soldier son and his soldier wife, were often deployed at the same time in different states or countries. They just had a baby girl, their only child. They could not leave the baby with just anyone, so I became their babysitter, which I fully enjoyed. I could work in any US military Hospitals or VA's Hospital and even Native American Indian Hospitals for they were under Federal Laws. Sometimes I worked three to nine months depending on the number of prescriptions where the hospital is behind. I did that when I am not babysitting. When one of them could stay home, I would work as a "pharmacist on call." One of my dreams is to see all the states in which I was able to accomplished. My mails were directed to my other son's address in California, and he gave me calls if something urgent came in the mail. He said that he did not believe one mailed envelop was urgent since it all came as an ordinary mail, not certified mail. This mail from Paul came after my two years of retirement

In the meantime, I had failed to find out where Paul was, since his friends said he now lived in various places and that he kept moving to different addresses. That was the main reason I lost my contact with Paul. Per his friends, he had been suspended, so he did not go to work.

Paul had become very sick, as those who knew him told me, but he could not enter the facility where he worked or even other VA facilities, for Paul had no money because his pay had been suspended. Soon his friends and office mates lost contact.

Paul was such a good man, full of laughter and a love of veterans, for he himself was a veteran. He loved this country, and he showed this love as a soldier in the Vietnam War, working hard, and being a whistleblower. I felt pain and grief, for I was not able to give a helping hand in his predicament, not knowing how to contact him. I tried to locate him several times but failed most of the time, as I was out of the state. Most of his friends did not know where he lives now, as they too lost contact. At last, I heard from one of his friends, and I was told that Paul died one year after I retired.

I prayed daily for him, Joe G, and Mary R, who were both victims too, that the Lord would bring them to eternal glory. I believe that, being good people, they are with the Maker now.

Laurence Paul Pinheiro, commonly known as Paul, was maltreated and denied his rights to be treated in the VA, even when he got seriously sick. Being a veteran, he had the right to be treated. These people who were responsible for the misery of many should be punished and even put in prison. But who could fight the powerful?

The hero, the veteran, the whistleblower who worked so hard, he was integrity himself. He was sent to his grave early, due to maltreatment, harassment, suspensions, and being escorted out from the VA by the VA Police. His prescriptions were not filled, and many rebuked him for reporting to the IG. He once asked me, "Could you tell me why God spared me during the Vietnamese War? My buddies were all around me floating in the river, and I purposely stood up to be hit while firing my weapon. I didn't want to be a prisoner. I kept on reloading and firing my weapon. No bullet hit me until succor came." Well, Paul, I now know the answer to your question. God made you the guardian of the VA, and you were able to get back stolen money and have the guilty imprisoned.

Chapter 7
Union President of Three States

Meantime, Wise Turtle, the pharmacy technician who was the friend of the president of the union, was becoming the officer of the union. He studied everything concerning the union, so when the union president retired, he became the president in California within a year. He then resigned as a pharmacy technician. The second year, he became president of the union in Nevada, and after another year, he was the president of the union in Arizona. All in all, Wise Turtle became the president of the union in three states: California, Nevada, and Arizona.

Several times, the secretary of the Veteran's Affairs would come to our facility to tell us his agenda to improve the services of the VA. The former pharmacy technician, a pharmacist subordinate who was now president of the union of three states, was often on the stage together with the secretary of Veterans Affairs. He was now dressed in expensive designer attires and wearing $400.00 shoes per his friends. Rumor has it that he had a very expensive house in Chino Hills. He would look at us smiling, and it seemed like he was saying, "I am up here, and you are down there." We were all happy for him.

THE BOMBSHELL

3 face prison in ▇▇▇ drug case

▶ **Loma Linda:** They are guilty of stealing $280,000 in medical drugs from hospitals for resale in a drug store.

LOMA LINDA
Three men, including a former pharmacist at the Loma Linda ▇▇ hospital and an accomplice who sold him drugs taken from the hospital, face sentencing next year on conspiracy to commit theft charges, officials said.

The case wrapped up Monday after New Jersey pharmacist ▇▇ who left the ▇▇ Medical Center in 1989, pleaded guilty to selling $280,000 worth of drugs that he knew had been stolen from hospitals in Loma Linda and East Orange, N.J. He and business partner ▇▇ sold the drugs in a drugstore they owned.

▇▇, assistant U.S. attorney, said that during the time ▇▇ worked at the Loma Linda hospital, he met ▇▇ a pharmacy technician. Hospital officials confirmed that an ▇▇ worked as a pharmacy technician and quit in 1995.

▇▇ said ▇▇ stole a variety of drugs including AZT, a drug used by AIDS patients, Procardia, a drug that treats hypertension, and buspar, a drug that treats anxiety. The assistant U.S. attorney said ▇▇ was taking boxes of drugs that were received as shipments and sending them to the New Jersey drugstore.

Between 1993 and 1995, ▇▇ shipped 55 packages of drugs worth between $800 and $4,600 apiece to ▇▇ in New Jersey. ▇▇ was paid about half of the retail value of each shipment, ▇▇ said.

She said ▇▇ pleaded guilty last year to conspiracy to steal government property and faces up to five years in prison as well as fines. He, along with ▇▇ and ▇▇ face sentencing next year.

▇▇ said investigators received a tip two years ago that drugs were being stolen at veterans' facilities in New Jersey and Loma Linda.

▇▇ who was hired last month as chief of pharmacy at the hospital said the staff was not aware of an investigation or that drugs were being stolen.

▇▇ said that for at least the last five years, VA hospitals nationwide have had stringent policies to prevent theft of drugs that have a potential for abuse. None of the drugs mentioned by ▇▇ fit that category, ▇▇ said.

▇▇ said she is reviewing pharmacy procedures and will recommend any necessary changes.

"That will be interesting to know whether it was elaborate or very simplified, either way it will be something that we can correct," she said.

One day in June, I opened a newspaper in San Bernardino County in California while eating breakfast to find big news: "PRESIDENT OF THE UNION OF THREE STATES ARRESTED."

I was shocked. I kept on reading. Wise Turtle had been arrested, along with two pharmacists in New York for stealing drugs from the VA hospital. One was a former pharmacist who worked with Wise Turtle in the same VA hospital for several years and then quit when he went to live in New York. He opened a drugstore with another pharmacist who was also arrested. The first newspaper stated that Wise Turtle was union president of three states. Later, it was no longer mentioned that he was the president of the union but that he was a former pharmacy technician. The union maybe removed his records of being president of the union in three states.

The result of the inspector general investigation proved that drugs were stolen and sent to New York. The one who committed the crime was Wise Turtle, who was the pharmacy technician at the time. The inspector general took three years investigating, while Wise Turtle was becoming the union president of California, Nevada, and Arizona. He was in cahoots with two pharmacists, one who was a former employee with the same facility and another pharmacist from New York. Both pharmacists owned a drugstore in New York, where the drugs were being sold.

In August 1997, another newspaper in the same county also mentioned, "THE RESULTS OF IG'S INVESTIGATION." Now, this reminds me of what my father said to us, his children: "The one who did something in the dark will always come to light. Never compromise your future by doing bad." Wise Turtle's success came crashing down, and I believed it would be hard for him to recover. However, Wise Turtle was relieved, as he was union president, and he did not go to prison. He was on house arrest per pharmacy staff. According to those who knew him, the union lawyer helped him. The two pharmacists were imprisoned for three years and lost their pharmacy license. The three of them were also penalized to pay the amount of the stolen drugs, as the two newspapers reported.

The VA was able to get back the stolen money, which was around $280,000.00. The whistleblower reported to the inspector general to investigate why the drugs were being sent to New York when our territory was only from Barstow to San Diego.

A member of the personnel from the accounting department often comes to me fanning a check from Wise Turtle. He is paying for the stolen drugs.

Chapter 8
Suffering as a Victim

Power corrupts, and coupled with a mean woman's love, it will seek to destroy.

It was proven that VA employees of a special ethnic group gained many privileges, such as receiving computers to work in their homes, which was not allowed at that time. They were also granted to attend continuing education classes sponsored by the VA without penalizing their leave time. Annual leave was not deducted for them, but mine was, and some staff with the same grade were charged annual leave. This behavior showed bias. The employees in the special group were also given easy jobs, where they worked with lots of help while the other workers were instructed to work alone to cope with the long lines of patients waiting for outpatient services. The inpatient pharmacy was also loaded with many prescriptions since only one pharmacist was on duty, usually the targeted ones. The usual pattern of work in the inpatient pharmacy was one or two pharmacists would work to keep up with new orders where the intravenous (IV) medication from doctors' orders from different floors were coming. Pharmacists who worked on those floors input the orders. One technician was assigned to the IV room where intravenous medications are being prepared. The IV room is a big sterilized section of the Pharmacy. There is also the PO sections meaning any medicine given by mouth, such as pills ,capsules and liquid and any other medications that can be taken by mouth.

In the PO section were other shelves, medications applied to the skin, such as creams, suppositories and any other medications were displayed. EYE and EAR medications were also in other shelves. The "special people" often had extra pharmacists to help when lots of orders were pouring in from other floors. This service was denied to the pharmacist who the Big Viper wanted to get rid of. This clearly showed preferential treatment within the managerial consistency in the oversight of professional staff with such magnitude in responsibility.

WHEN DID THE "FRAME UP" START?

As documented, the activities of every pharmacist were in the computer data. My supervisor planned to destroy me for he hated me for filing a EEO case. He attempted to print a picture of excessive mistakes that he claimed I had made when processing medication orders. He attempted to state that I did not follow regulations, including nonexistent regulations.

I had been a pharmacist at the Veterans Hospital for more than eight years before the "frame up" started. I was always a cheerful person, for I loved my work. There were pharmacists' mandatory meetings usually at seven o'clock in the morning for the purpose of updating on what is new in Pharmacy. Here new drugs were discussed, their side effects if any, and other problems that occur in caring for patients. When I come in pharmacy technicians and medical interns were already working. As I said, when Mr. Dick was the director, the atmosphere was always a happy one. When the acting pharmacy director, King Shorty, whom staff believed considered himself a king, took over, the environment of the pharmacy drastically changed. The staff then worked quietly, and most had frowns on their faces. I would come in and ask, "Who is dead?"

The answer was always, "We are all dead, but we all have resurrected since you are here now." Everybody then began laughing, including me. They asked, "Why are you laughing?"

I answered, "Because I am the happiest woman in the world, and you all should be happy too." Silently, I prayed, "Lord, help all of us. Give us all the strength to overcome this fear of losing our jobs." The next day, I was given a shirt by the pharmacy staff with a bold print, which read, "The Happiest Person in the World."

I respected and cared for everyone, especially the veterans who were working at the VA, for they were the best of men and women, both in character and in their love and service to this country. I have seen this wonderful character countless times in their tireless work and in their interactions with their fellow veterans who were our patients. These were veterans who had served their country in their youth and were being replace by non-veteran employees who came from another country and did not speak English fluently.

I believe because of her status, the Queen Bee always received preferential treatment from the staff. Co-workers stepped aside to let her pass, and a path was given everywhere she went. During meetings, one was always ready to vacate a seat for her. At parties, she was the first one to be served.

I was not aware of these actions until later. I was in the canteen, just finishing my break, when somebody behind called me; I turned around to look. In front of me was the Chosen One, and she looked furious with blazing eyes. I asked her, "What is the matter?" I didn't know why she was angry.

She put her fingers in front of my face and said, "Get out of my way." Her fingers were near my eyes, so I lifted my right hand and pushed her fingers away from my face. I said her name gently, then added, "We are in public place, and we will talk about whatever it is that made you angry in the pharmacy."

In a very loud voice, sounding like she wanted attention, she said, "I don't want to talk to you." She was with two of her countrywomen, as well as the countrywomen of the pharmacist supervisor, Cobra. They could be witnesses against me.

I was upset, so I went down to King Shorty's office to let him know what had happened. I told him what occurred between the

Chosen One and me in detail. He said, "If you don't want it here, quit; it's better."

I was so speechless at this employee harassment that I could not move. Then I said, "Why, I have worked here for more than eight years, and there is no complaint about me."

He then said, "Just go out," which I did, perplexed at why I was treated that way.

I prayed, "Lord, You were spit upon, slapped many times, rejected by many, nothing in comparison to this treatment I just received. I will just forget it happened."

Even then, I was not aware of the gossip about the chosen one. Again, I did not mind the incident, but I became conscious of my environment. I noticed the attraction between the acting pharmacy director and the Chosen One. I believed everyone presumed that Mr. Shorty was in love with the Chosen One because of their behavior and preferential treatment. In retrospect, I think that she deliberately confronted me and wanted a fight in the canteen. If I had acted differently, the acting director would have had reason to fire me. I believed she wanted me to be fired so that another pharmacist who belonged to the same ethnic group as hers could replace me.

Chapter 9

Cobra

My supervisor, secretly named "Cobra," was working **three** jobs for twenty-four hours daily. He worked eight hours in the VA, then swing shift eight-hour shifts at a local hospital. Most of the time, I was acting pharmacist supervisor. Cobra made the schedule so that when the midnight pharmacist was off, or if the other pharmacist was on midnight duties or on sick leave or vacation, he changed the schedules of these workers. Then he worked the midnight shift, including weekends. He was so tired from working multiple employment that he left beddings in the fourth floor pharmacy satellite. He would sleep there. In the morning, we would remove his beddings because it was a job site and used to dispense drugs for inpatients. When he was tired, he would call me in the wee hours of two or three o'clock in the morning to go to work. I was not scheduled to work when these calls came, yet I always obliged to his call. I did not realize I was about to be discriminated at that moment. I always came because of my love for work, and my son being a soldier gave me an affinity for the people we served. He told me that since I lived nearby the VA, it was just fitting that I took over his work while he was away. The technicians answered the phones and prepared the necessary medications while Cobra slept, an **oversight** of a registered pharmacist job. When I came in, I checked the accumulated technicians' work and took over as the pharmacist. Everybody in the pharmacy staff knew that Cobra worked an equivalent of twenty-four hours a day, which included duties on weekends.

My supervisor, Cobra, was dismissed from one of the local hospitals where he was working swing shift, due to some "narcotic discrepancy." My friend said that he had stolen a big quantity of narcotics (schedule-two drugs) while on duty. The one who dismissed him was a very good friend of mine and was then the Pharmacy Director of the said hospital. One day, Cobra called me into his office to ask me if I had seen the director who had dismissed him. I answered in the negative, for my friend had never mentioned the dismissal. Also, I had not seen my friend lately. He talked with me about the director, saying that she was a nice lady, very caring and efficient. I just listened as he kept on talking about her and praising her. He stated that she was a very talented lady and a super director. I was puzzled at the conversation but said nothing. He then told me to **forget** what we had talked about, and he asked me to shake hands with him, which I did. Afterwards, I came to believed that he had talked about the director who fired him to be sure that I did not relay his dismissal to our staff. At the time, however, I had no knowledge of the dismissal. I later realized that he was an inveterate liar and an incorrigible thief. My friend never mentioned the dismissal to me until I told her about my EEO case.

Cobra also destroyed the reputation of a good honest man, Joe G. He saved himself, for he was afraid of losing his job, and also because he was trying to get a position in saddling with the vicious King Shorty. Cobra eventually became very close with the acting pharmacy director.

Together, they persecuted, harassed, intimidated and even did bodily harm to their subordinates whom they want to get rid of. Two senior pharmacists were even forced to retire and were replaced by the special ethnic group who spoke pidgin English. These two cruel high-ranking officers promised jobs to pharmacy interns and studying pharmacy technicians, as well as promotions to new employees if they agreed to become spies to those whom both wanted to get rid of. Many of these individuals told me how King Shorty and Cobra had no morals and that they would not lower themselves to such levels. Some, though, decided to become traitors.

Chapter 10
The Undesirables

The Pharmacy Director, Ronald Dick retired. Mr. Shorty, the former assistant Pharmacy Director, became the Acting Pharmacy Director . A big change in management occurred. The pharmacy employees spoke to each other in whispers and worked quietly, smiles were few, and the days dragged on slowly. One could see the old personalities of these co-workers only during breaks and at lunch time, when they were free to laugh and joke with one another.

Yet many green forest snakes came to rest in their fields, devouring and destroying those who opposed them. They abused others, while using their power to annihilate their presumed enemies—the oppressed ones, the former-soldiers-turned-employees, the Undesirables. They became the target of discrimination, harassment, and maltreatment. The main goal of these powerful people, whom employees secretly called "the Snakes," was to terminate the jobs of the Undesirables, the source of their livelihood. Most Undesirables, if not all, had families to feed. King Shorty, also secretly called "the Big Viper," disregarded the excellent performance of the Undesirables, as evidenced by stellar approved reports and their dedication to veterans. The three most powerful in the pharmacy department were the pharmacist supervisor, whom many called Cobra; one member of the federal union named the Rattle Snake; and the acting pharmacy director, who was called the Big Viper.

Cobra lived in the next subdivision where I lived, only a ten-minute walk from my place. Once in a while, before my EEO case, he would pass by my home with his two children, so they knew me pretty well. Several times, he would bring his kids to the Pharmacy satellite during office hours and asked me to watch them for a while. Being a neighbor, I could not refuse after seeing to it that the pharmacy activity was in a lull. The staff even laughed in accusing me of brownnosing. I just laughed together with them, for it was not true and they know it too.

These three people—the Big Viper, Cobra, and the Rattle Snake, humiliated, scorned, framed, harassed, and even inflicted bodily harm on the undesirables. They rained verbal insults and threatening words and created false evidences on VA forms approved by the powerful themselves. They attempted to eradicate the good performance that these so-called Undesirables accomplished. These were the acceptable techniques that the powerful employed to devastate their subordinates' wellbeing, both psychological and physiological. Employees feared these powerful people, for they did harm in many different ways. The powerful enlisted the help of the weaker or those with similar thinking to help them by spying the activities of the Undesirables. Those who wanted increases in their salaries helped them in their atrocities. Unhappily, some union representatives conniving with them who were also subordinates of Big Viper, as well as some registry workers who wanted to get a job with the government, helped them in their evil deeds. The Big Viper did these actions because he was planning to replace the undesirables in their positions with the ones in the special ethnic group which he favored.

Chapter 11
The Victims

THE FIRST VICTIM: LAURENCE PAUL PINHEIRO – THE WHISTLEBLOWER
THE SECOND VICTIM: JOE G.– PHARMACIST

*J*oe G. worked with this VA for many, many years. He was a very decent, helpful person to everybody. He was known as "the beloved pharmacist." He was loved and respected by co-workers and other departments as well. He was one of the best employees, and he worked very hard; he was always dedicated in his work and caring for his co-workers and the veterans he served. He helped countless people who came to him for advice, and he aided them with problematic issues and securing better jobs. He was a mentor to **all** new employees at the pharmacy, teaching each one the system on how the pharmacy works. Everyone who knew him loved, respected, and admired him.

He was told to retire, for he was the friend of the whistleblower, the Undesirables, and even some department heads. Many believed that the Big Viper wanted his position to be vacant so that he could replace him with someone of the favored ethnic group. He was about fifty-five years old when he was accused of stealing **one bottle** of cough syrup with codeine. It was a big shock for everybody. He could easily have asked for a prescription from some physician friends, for he was a smoker. He was a veteran and entitled to the medicine for treatment and free medication with a small amount of co-pay. He needed the cough syrup. **Cobra told Joe G. not to bother, since it was not a schedule-two drug. Cobra himself gave the bottle of cough syrup in the presence of many staff in the pharmacy.** Joe G. was told to retire and that he would not be reported to the State Board of Pharmacy. The witnesses told Joe G. that they would witness for him. He rejected, saying, "I have a higher position than you guys, and they can do this to me. You have your family to think about, and anyway, I can easily get a job outside since they will not report me to the Board of Pharmacy."

About this time, King Shorty was trying to find pharmacist spots for Chosen One's friends to work in the VA Hospital. That included outside jobs since the Viper wanted people in the special ethnic group to procure jobs. Joe G. had several grandchildren to support. Their mother had just died, and Joe G. was helping his family. The news was that Joe G. was reported to the Pharmacy Board anyway, so he could not even work part time, as his license had been revoked.

Joe G. died due to stress and shame with the thought that people believed him to be a thief. In the funeral church service, the whole pharmacy staff except the ones on duty and the special ethnic group were there. Also, many from other departments attended. Several were teary-eyed and openly crying. Then in came Cobra. Several men stood up to block his entrance. One said, "Your presence is a poison to everybody here, especially the family of our friend who just left us. Please leave, or we will throw you out."

Soon a commotion ensued. Shouting and physical confrontation was about to occur, for Cobra did not want to leave. The priest intervened. He said, "Please respect our friend and his family." Cobra sat down in an empty bench, and many angry eyes were focused on him. After a while, he finally left. Of course, Joe G.was eventually replaced by a pharmacist who belonged to the **special ethnic group.**

I asked myself, "Where is justice?" How about Cobra, who was dismissed by my best friend, the director of the pharmacy department where he was working swing shift? The record shows he stole **lots** of narcotics **(schedule-two drugs).** Yet he was not reported to the State Board of Pharmacy. Joe G.was in possession of **one bottle of cough syrup,** not even a schedule-two drug. This bottle of cough syrup was even handed to him by Cobra, and many witnesses saw this take place. Where is justice?

THE THIRD VICTIM: MARY R– PHARMACY TECHNICIAN

Cobra was influenced by the union representative nicknamed Rattle Snake. This person was called Rattle Snake for a reason. When he first came to the VA as a pharmacy technician, his livelihood was not stable. He had two young children, and his wife was not working. One pharmacy technician, Mary R who was kindhearted and had lots of assets, decided to help him. She brought Rattle Snake to work and took him back home, for he didn't have a car. Mary R also lent him money for rent and food. When he could not pay back the loans from Mary R, they were just forgiven. This happened for almost a year, until he became stable in his livelihood and his wife started working.

Mary R treated Rattle Snake like her own son, until his wife got a job. Since his wife was in the same ethnic group as the union president, she got a supervisor job in the VA store. At last, Rattle Snake was able to buy a car. Still, he had no gratitude, and he even helped persecute Mary R.when she applied for EEO. Mary R.was the guardian of the pharmacy vault, did the inventories, and monitored the narcotic records, doubly checking that everything was correct. She had been doing this for eighteen years. Although she had been paying her union dues, Mary R was written up for the first time, harassed many times, and transferred to a more difficult job where she had to be trained. She was even timed while learning. She was written up almost weekly. All this happened because Mary R.had lots of friends, the friends of the whistleblower, many who began to oppose King Shorty's management—the Undesirables. The pharmacy staff believed that the main reason King Shorty wanted to vacate Mary R's position of eighteen years was that he desired to hire a "brownnose person" who would alter narcotic records so that King Shorty and Cobra could manipulate and change narcotic records done by any pharmacist they wanted to get rid of. They succeeded in transferring Mary R.to a new job.

During Mary R.'s EEO application interview, Rattle Snake testified against her. He came to me and told me about it. I said, "How in the world you could you do such a thing after all the love and help she bestowed on you?" He then ran back to the interviewing officer to redact his testimony. The officer wouldn't allow it, saying that it had already been recorded. Mary R.waited for a hearing on her case. Meanwhile, her every move was constantly watched, whether she is late, she stayed too long on break, or she socialized while working. They watched who she talked to her during office hours, and when she used the telephone, they monitored who she called and whether the calls were job related.

Friends of Queen Bee stated that Mary R. was crocheting in her office. True, she was crocheting sweaters for Rattles Snake's children, but she did this while on her break. She found out later that the lawyer the union gave her was a friend of Rattle Snake, and her hearings were always cancelled at different times for different reasons.

These happenings took a toll on Mary R.'s health, and she died without a hearing and had paid her union dues for twenty-one years while working. My heart was heavy with guilt. I thought to myself, *Am I one of the causes of her problem for being a friend of hers?* Mary R. was a friend of many, mostly the Undesirables. She was loved by many, as shown at her funeral. Lots of people came, even from different departments, including the whole pharmacy staff except those who were on duty and the cronies of Queen Bee. Many were visibly crying, for everyone who worked with Mary R and knew her loved her.

I would pray, "Lord, bring them to everlasting life, where they will be happy with You." I still pray daily for Mary R, Paul, and Joe G.

THE FOURTH VICTIM: DON K– PHARMACY TECHNICIAN AND VETERAN:

Don K had been working the second shift since he had started sixteen years prior. He was also a veteran and an exemplary employee.

He became a member of the Undesirables since he was a friend of the whistleblower, Joe G, Mary R, myself, many veteran co-employees in the same department, and many veterans who were working in the hospital. He too became a victim. His schedule was changed to the dayshift, so he had to pay for a babysitter, which his family could not afford. This gave him lots of distress and destroyed his peaceful life. He did not want to look for another job, for he would be losing his retirement pay, which would have been available to him in four years. Usually, he did not owe any money, yet he was now forced to borrow from friends and credit companies. Soon his health became a problem, and the last I heard, he was on disability.

Chapter 12

Harassment

Even now, I am still baffled as to why I became a victim in this situation. I don't know what I did wrong. The only reason I could presume is that I didn't belong to the same ethnic group as the Chosen One and Mr. Shorty, who wanted to change the pharmacy population to suit their ethnic group. Another reason might be my encounter with the Chosen One when she was applying for a job, which I completely forgot; God knows I told no one about it. It could be, she started resenting being now called the "Chosen One" for co-staff were starting to avoid her.

I believed my supervisor wanted to get outstanding grades, which was why he was always associated with the acting pharmacy director. Then strange occurrences started to happen. When procuring narcotics from the pharmacy vault, the usual procedure for the inpatient pharmacist was to leave a note for the vault technician, Mary R's domain, to advise her which drug was taken and the quantity of it. Most of the time, this occurred during weekends, swing shift, or the midnight schedule. This made the vault technician aware of what drug and the quantity was taken from the pharmacy inventory. The law states that the pharmacist should enter drugs taken in a log book, but since there was always only one pharmacist on duty in the inpatient pharmacy on weekends, it was not reasonable to stay away longer, for there might have been a code blue where the pharmacist should be present. That had been the norm for the more than **eight years** I had been working as a pharmacist. The vault technician was allowed to enter narcotics in the log book since she was the presumed guardian of the vault; this also made her aware of what drugs were taken during nights and weekends. During daytime office hours, there was **always** a vault pharmacist in the vault who checked the daily entry and tally done by the vault technician. Throughout the normal office hours, the vault technician would deliver the narcotics for the inpatient pharmacy to the pharmacist in charge in the inpatient pharmacy, who would record the items into the inpatient narcotic log Book. When a night pharmacist went home early or could not come to work, the supervisor would usually call me to work in their place. Many times, I also acted as the Pharmacist Supervisor during the day shift when he was not around since he had multiple jobs. I did not mind doing this, since my two children were not home. One was in college and the other was in the army, and my husband worked in Bakersfield. Therefore, since I was alone, I preferred to work, especially because I lived within five minutes of the hospital.

One day, King Shorty called for me, and my supervisor, Cobra, was there too. Both said that I did not log the narcotics in the log book twice during the past **weekends.** I was dumbfounded. "Nobody told me that there was a change in the procedure," I said. **That day,** the procedure was changed to state that all pharmacists should log entries in the log book in the vault, even on nights and on weekends. **The write-ups had been done before the change in**

procedure. My supposed negligence was still recorded and written up as mistakes. However, I did not pay much attention to this because I did not have any inkling that both my supervisor and the acting pharmacy director wanted to get rid of me.

Meanwhile, two senior pharmacists were told to quit or retire. They could not bear being watched all the time and being written up for false accusations. There was no punch clock, yet they were told they were always late, even though they would come in on time. I later found out that they had been constantly harassed, so they decided to quit. This was necessary because if they were fired, they might have lost their pharmacy license.

I never got an outstanding grade on my evaluations. On all my evaluations, all items were always graded as outstanding except **one** item, different at all times, would have an above average grade. This prevented me from getting an outstanding grade. My performance was superior on all of the items.

After a week, the acting director called me into his office again. This was concerning another mistake which I did not do: the narcotic inventory did not tally. **The best way to destroy a pharmacist is to show his or her incompetence in dealing with narcotics. A pharmacist's trustworthiness then becomes questionable. I became suspicious, as I had been written up twice in two weeks, so I filed a complaint with EEO.** My father often told us his children, "It is better for a man to be dead than live without honor." If I got fired, it would devastate my father and my family. I learned later, my supervisor was scared he would be demoted, since he was always away working with other hospitals. He was afraid that I would take his place per some staff. That was the reason I got another "write-up"

COMPUTER TAMPERING

In the pharmacy, the computer generated copies of orders and documents. The pharmacist's actions for every order were documented in the computer when the pharmacist entered the medical doctor's order, so the computer was the best record of a pharmacist performance. However, computer problems were endless and often could not be solved. Management stated they didn't know the reasons why the computer system went down so often, and most breakdowns happened when I was on duty. The breakdowns accumulates more orders and more jobs. Nobody should know anybody's access code, yet my code was used while I was off duty. I found out that my access code was being used by two pharmacy technician spies; one was Rattle Snake and the other was called the Sidekick. Rattle Snake was now a union representative, and his wife belonged to the same ethnic group of the union president. The Sidekick was the new pharmacy computer coordinator, a former pharmacy technician who was just promoted for the position.

THE TRAITORS

Two registry workers, BK and KL, who wanted a job with the VA, were told to write me up, and they did. The letter they wrote stated that I was mean and that I shouted to them and called them "useless." I asked them why they did this, after I had been very nice to them and had helped them a lot. They told me that they had been promised a job by King Shorty and Cobra.

BEING BLAMED

One day, I was blamed for lost pharmacy master keys, even though I was not there when it happened. I was written up for this. The Queen Bee lost the keys twice, and at one time, she lost the keys for a month. Management even had to change all the pharmacy locks, and the cost was $10,000.00 per accounting department. Of course, nothing happened to her—no write-ups.

MALTREATMENT

The hospital had passed the JCHO inspection. For the whole month, I stayed in the nursing home many times until two o'clock in the morning to study the profiles of patients while doing the necessary documentation, which had not been done by the previous pharmacist assigned there. We were a team—doctors, nurses, dieticians, and dentist. All of them got outstanding awards, and they told me I would surely get one too. So, when King Shorty and Cobra called me in for a meeting, I was expecting an award or at least a pat on the back. Instead, both treated me like dirt. In King Shorty's office, the two of them were ogling at me. King Shorty handed me his pen and a write-up dated July 19, 1995, about errors involving green sheets (narcotics). The write-up was dated **June 13, 1995,** and the offense supposedly occurred on **June 25,1995.** What a **big blunder** for both of them. The write-up had already been written, and the mistake was claimed to have been done on June 25, 1995, before it happened. I have a suspicion of who tampered with the green sheet errors: Rattle Snake. He was so powerful that all pharmacy technicians he recommended were accepted by

Cobra and King Shorty. When I didn't want to sign the document because it was not true, both became very angry, and their faces became so red. King Shorty grabbed the pen from my hand and **signed my name.** By law, nobody has the right to sign someone else's name, especially if that person objects and the document was falsified. This was forgery. The award I was supposed to receive turned into a write-up.

DENIED AWARDS

No awards were given to me, while a mother and daughter who just barely came in were given bonuses. Of course, it was the Chosen One and her daughter. Her son was also hired the same time as her daughter, but he was told to quit because it was unlawful due to conflict of interest. Another pharmacist who belonged to the same ethnic group as them was hired and was given award after just being hired.

Two pharmacist in Queen Bee's ethnic group, and also one of whom was from the same country as Cobra, were sent to New Orleans for continuing education class. They got free plane tickets, hotels, and more. It was not announced, but the staff found out when these individuals came back.

DENIED OPPORTUNITY

Quality assurance jobs were given to those in the special ethnic groups, and one was from the same place as Cobra. They monitored the pharmacist entry on prescriptions and looked for mistakes. I volunteered to be one, and of course, I was denied.

Chapter 13

The Violence

After I applied for EEO, my attitude reverted back to the old me. I was happy in my job and put everything in God's hands. I still worked hard and got along with everybody. I believed I didn't have any enemies, so the days were the same, sometimes hectic and sometimes with a lull in the workplace. Cobra came from a country where women were **not** considered equal to men, per one of his countrywomen who was also working with us. Twice in conversations, I heard Cobra say, **"It is only my mother." I cringed at this, for to me, my mother is the most important person, respected, honored, and loved by my family. As the norm in USA, women are love and respected.** Cobra had already lived here for many years, so he should have known that women have the same rights as men and are honored, especially in this country. This same countrywoman of his told us also that even young girls were raped and that it's always the girl's fault when this happens.

I was not aware that my supervisor, Cobra, was seething in anger due to my filing a complaint with the EEO office. Within a week after I applied for EEO, around ten o'clock in the morning, some staff went on break. I was left behind in the pharmacy with two pharmacy technicians. My supervisor came in and stood very near me, and I believed then that he was checking what I was inputting in the computer. I noticed he seemed to be looking around, which should have been usual, for he was perhaps looking at the inventories on the pharmacy bins. He asked about my soldier son and if he knew karate. **I replied, "Of course," and suddenly, Cobra hit me on the temple.** I nearly lost consciousness. Even when I was a child, nobody had ever hit me, even while playing rough games. Baffled, I dizzily walked to another computer away from him. For a long time, I was dazed. The pharmacy became very quiet until the employees on breaks came back. Cobra had physically assaulted me. **A man hitting a defenseless woman is the scum of the earth.**

I should have gone to the ER, but I did not because I was still disoriented and had lost the ability to decide. The two technicians who had witnessed the assault said that they could be my witnesses if I needed them. However, I could not ask them to be witnesses, for I was ranked much higher than they and their jobs might also have been in jeopardy. I had to consider their families, so I let it go.

My headache persisted the whole night, so the next day, I went to the employee health department, and the doctor who saw me gave me some pain pills and sent me home to rest. The doctor came from the same country as Cobra, so she did not report the incident. **This is dereliction of duty.** In recollection, I believe Cobra did not want me to apply for EEO because both he and King Shorty wanted me to quit or be fired. But I was brought up to stand up for what is right and fight for it if necessary.

My supervisor deserved the name Cobra for striking a defenseless woman; his action was outrageous. He had the character of the lowest human being on earth. An animal fights and kills only when hungry, but this Cobra was worse than any animal. He hit me without provocation. His actions, including what he did to Joe G, are reprehensible. Thus, I prayed, "Lord, give me strength and keep me under Your care, and guide me in what is best to do."

I did not inform my family of the incident. My soldier son was then deployed in a dangerous place, and I didn't want him to worry about me. When given the chance, he would surely seek and confront my supervisor and would make him pay for what he had done to me. My other son is a champion in Thai-chi and karate, and he had lots of friends who specialized in defense systems; so, I did not tell him either. Both of my sons were college graduates and well versed in self-defense. If they knew a cruel person had attacked their mother, they would not stop in seeking him, for they love me very much. I have never told them the name of my supervisor, Cobra, **even now**. Nobody in my family knew the trouble I was in. **I relied on God's help, for I knew He would never abandon me.**

Chapter 14

A Patient Died

The pharmacists were responsible for putting doctors' orders in the computer. They are the ones who to see to it that everything is in compliance with the doctors' orders. Also, they check the conditions of the patient's health, reviewing the patient's profile, age, height, weight, liver and kidney functions, and overall health conditions. They also check the previous drug orders, doses, strengths of drug use, frequency of the doses, how the patient is responding to the treatment, and many other things related to the patient's wellbeing.

One day, as I came across one patient, I immediately found out that the new **drug order dose given was too high.** The pharmacist who did this was **Queen Bee.** I checked and rechecked, and the conclusion was that the dose given was too high. Could it be that the manufacturer had given a new dose to the drug? To be sure, I called the State Board of Pharmacy, and I was right: the dose was too high. It should have been much lower. I ran to the patient's room to retrieve the medication that was to be given intravenously, hoping it had not yet been given. The nurse said that the patient had just died after receiving the medication. The pharmacist who did this was careless and inefficient, and thus killed the patient. It was the precious Queen Bee.

Chapter 15
Applying for a Supervisor Job

During King Shorty's term, the outpatient pharmacy supervisor position became vacant many times. One of my best friends visited me one day, and I informed her that the outpatient pharmacy supervisor's office was vacant. She started laughing and said that the two of us should apply to find out who was the better between us. We always joked with one another in many ways. She was a black lady with a PhD degree in Pharmacy, as well as a veteran; I, on the other hand, was just a licensed pharmacist with regular experience. **My friend said that she would not apply if I didn't apply.** I was happy in my job and content, and I had no desire to be a supervisor at that time. Due to her insistence, we both applied for the open position. She had the quality of a very good supervisor, and the veterans would have better care if she was hired for the role. We laughed our heads off, for both of us were denied, just as we had expected.

We even celebrated by eating out, for we had already known the outcome before it happened, as the acting director only hired the special ethnic group of the Chosen One. Again, a pharmacist belonging to the special ethnic group was hired. She was accepted even though her experience was minimal in comparison to my friend and myself. **She did not last long.** After four months, she quit, and the position was open again. Both of our applications were **still active and on file, but we were never interviewed.** A new white pharmacist became the new supervisor, and many were happy, as improvements did occur. We were all happy, for she was very efficient and treated the staffs impartially. However, the new outpatient supervisor quit early, and many were disappointed since she was well liked. The rumor was that she did not like the management environment.

A university was located near the VA hospital where I worked. Many medical interns and PhD Pharmacy students from different universities around the country did their internships at this VA hospital. Before, there were very few PhD graduates in Pharmacy, as this was a new program. So, regular licensed pharmacists in the VA became mentors for these medical and PhD Pharmacy students. Later, they worked with the VA with a PhD in Pharmacy, but I was once their teacher. I believed we still had the superior knowledge since we were in the field and also furthered our education through continuing education and special classes. Several times, **different university pharmacy professors from different states** came to give us lessons on updates about what was new in the profession. Classes were scheduled on weekends and lasted a year. Immediately afterwards, there were classes again. We received diplomas for these courses, mostly clinical subjects.

Deeply, I prayed, "Lord, Thy will be done, for I believe the best always happens in accordance to Your will."

Chapter 16
The Helpers

Often, when I was walking through the hospital corridors, employees from different departments would stop me and say, "Oh, I found the book you wanted to borrow, and it's here. You can read it and return it whenever you like." I was puzzled, for I didn't remember asking to borrow a book. In between the pages of the book were articles pertaining to my case. Many notes were inside, stating ugly incidents about Cobra and the many pharmacists within the special ethnic group. Lots were exasperated, for Cobra was not accessible when needed. The special ethnic group pharmacists were taking too long in providing medications for patients. Some incorrect drugs had even been given to nurses who would administer them to patients. It was good for the nurses to double check the medications before giving them to patients. However, many pharmacists had just come to the country and were not familiar with the medications. The Helpers, who were nurses, doctors, med.techs , and even a librarian, were willing to be witnesses in my favor if needed.

Paul invited me to a birthday party that coming Saturday. I told him, "But was not your birthday last month?" I remembered that we had eaten out with some pharmacy staff to celebrate his birthday.

"No, that was Elizabeth's b-day, my wife," he answered. Paul lived in an apartment not a mile away from the VA hospital, and he had a big space for parties. When I arrived for the party, almost all the inpatient pharmacy staff was already there except the ones on duty and friends of the Big Viper and Cobra. The party was a potluck, but I found out it was a meeting for the sake of my case. Some documents were copied and brought, especially the ones that involved the narcotics—where pharmacist just left notes for the vault technicians, which was the practice then—as well as copies of the original narcotic records. The old records showed how they had been tampered, and the new records, which I was supposed to have entered, revealed the discrepancy. Many entries were made, and Queen Bee had signed my name on them. There was also planning on how they would listen and copy documents that could be needed to support my case.

Lots of times after work, many of the pharmacy staff and other departments would go to Midnight Rodeo, one mile from the VA Hospital. There, employees learned cowboy dancing, exercises, and other different kinds of dances. We also used to eat dinner there because the food was cheap—it usually cost only $3.00 for a dinner with drinks and salad. Often, we only stayed until to seven o'clock at night. These meetings were so much fun because we were able to display our expertise in cowboy dancing. We all fell in line doing the Macarena, the Electric Slide, and other cowboy dances. We danced in complete abandonment, doing our best to outdo the others. Laughter was all around, and everybody really enjoyed the party. There was even a competition, and the winner was treated to a free dinner.

Afterwards, there were lots of jokes. The funniest one was when one of the boys pretend to be King Shorty and one girl tech was the Queen Bee. How the girl fluttered her long eyelashes (artificial of course), flirting with King Shorty, was really hilarious. The participants mimicked how King Shorty's walked and talked, and the girl copied even the dress, the diction, and the behavior of the Chosen One. She would sashay as she walked, and she even went behind a tree as King Shorty would follow slowly, looking around to be sure nobody was watching. Everybody pretended they were talking to one another and didn't notice the two as both disappear behind a tree. After a while, the woman appeared with a contented smile on her face, and she still walked with those sashaying steps. After a while, the man also came out wiping his red mouth, pretending to remove lipstick stains. We all laughed heartily, enjoying the show. I could not really describe how I felt at those moments—how people cared for me and went to such extremes to support me.

After that gathering, there were several parties to help me in my case. Many individuals gave me copies of my work, dates, and times, and they shared how they had been changed to make them appear to be mistakes. What bothered me was that their jobs might have also been in jeopardy.

Chapter 17
The Lawyer

I had the best lawyer during this time. He told me to just work as I usually did, while keeping quiet and recording all happenings every day. I had to report to him on anything unusual that occurred. I gathered all evidences, write-ups, all happenings and gave them to him. I also gave him all presumptive mistakes.

Chapter 18

The Trial

Introduction:

Pursuant to section 1614.109 of the commission's regulation, the administrative judge held a hearing on March 11, 12, 20, and 27, and April 3 and 15, 1997, at the Memorial Veterans Hospital in California on the discrimination complaint by Elisa Domingo Garcia against the Department of Veterans Affairs. Twenty-eight witnesses including the complainant testified at the hearing. Sixty-six exhibits were admitted into evidence.

THE HEARING

Witnesses:
The Most Notable Ones:

1. The Whistleblower: For trying to stop the thieving in the VA, he was hated, harassed, humiliated, and not permitted to enter the VA, where he worked. His testimony was discarded.

2. The Sidekick: He is the assistant of King Shorty. When called, he was trembling like a leaf. His face was so white, and when seated, he kept pounding at his thighs. He received promotions and became the computer coordinator to the pharmacy staff, after being sent to computer lessons. I believed he was the one who had given my password to the pharmacy employees who deliberately made mistakes on my behalf. I knew he was told to lie and was forced to do it or could lose his new job. I looked at the judge, and I saw pity in his eyes. The judge decided that the Sidekick was telling the truth. My question was, if one was telling the truth, why was he so afraid in the witness stand? He was a former soldier and should not have been scared to tell the truth.
3. LC: This was the technician who took over Mary R's job in the narcotic vault. She helped in messing the narcotic records to put blame on me. My entries in the Narcotic Log Book were altered and my name signed by Queen Bee. She was hated by many knowing her as a double face character and a friend of Big Viper. Co-workers were scared on what she will do to them. She was rewarded for being a brownnoser. The news was she got an outstanding grades in her evaluation.
4. DK: This was a friend of the whistleblower, and his testimony was also discarded. He too became a victim, and his swing shift job was changed to dayshift. Now he had to pay a babysitter for his children.
5. COBRA: This was the supervisor who had three jobs, working at two or three different hospitals daily, as well as on three different shifts and locations. He was an accomplice of the Big Viper, the acting pharmacy director, in harassing me. Also, he

violated me by punching me, a defenseless woman, without provocation. I don't know the outcome of his testimony.

6. OW: This was the doctor who came from the same country as Cobra. She did not report Cobra's attack against me. Of course, one had to side with and protect one's countrymen, and she disregarded her duty to report and told a lie about the reason I saw her. That is a dereliction of duty. "Lord, You were beaten a thousand times, and You accepted them in silence. Let me accept this, for I know Your justice will be done."

7. LS: This was a pharmacist of the same ethnic group as the complainant. She said she had been harassed several times and decided to quit. Her testimony was to be disregarded, even if she took the oath. She was replaced by someone in the special ethnic group.

8. TDR: She also took the oath, and her testimony was disregarded as well. When she went to see King Shorty to complain about one of the favored ethnic pharmacist who kept harassing her, King Shorty told her, "Why don't you commit suicide?" King Shorty admitted that he had said those words, but he told the judge that he had been only joking. What a joke! This statement was spoken after taking an oath. TDR retired, for she couldn't stand the atrocities done to her. A psych pharmacist (whose only task is to take care of psych patients, who are not many) was a very good friend of King Shorty, and he was promoted to GS 13. He pretended to slip and fall right on TDR, who belong to the same ethnic group as the complainant. She nearly fell and could have hit her head on a big stone block. The psych pharmacist hated our ethnic group and only cared for Queen Bee's special ethnic group. The staff believed that a

long time ago, he courted a lady belonging to the same ethnic group as complainant and was rejected. Well, he was despised by many, due to his superior attitude.

One time, I went to talk to the new interns with Cobra to enlighten them about the pharmacy policy of the VA, where I recommended some changes which King Shorty had approved. There is so many deficiencies in communications with the new Interns. In came the Psych Pharmacist who was very angry with me for talking to the new interns. This person did nothing but psych orders, yet he was promoted. Many of the pharmacy staff hated him, for he was a loner and acted just like King Shorty.

Chapter 19

Result of the EEO

*E*vidences were presented and accepted. Arguments on the qualifications of the complainant on being a supervisor were decided by the judge. The complainant has knowledge that was superior of the one who was accepted for the position, although she had a PhD. She was accepted simply because she belonged to the special ethnic group. Per the judge, the complainant had **double** experience as a pharmacist, but the PhD applicant was just a new graduate. I only partially won the case; I was promoted as a supervisor, which was effective beginning on the date on my supervisor application, and I was also given back pay as a supervisor from that date.

The other complaints were not justified based on ethnicity, sex, harassment, disparate treatment, and reprisal. The narcotic records tampered and the write-up per King Shorty were photographic errors. I believed the judge was not impartial as a federal employee; he sided with the VA administrator. Maybe he believed he was protecting the VA. To me, this was not right, for it would encourage bad managers to continue doing their evil deeds. This would eventually lessen the integrity of the VA. Also, the harassment, the assault, the humility, and the sufferings I encountered were not justified. I believed the only reason that I partly won the case was to prevent me from exposing the death of a patient.

The judge ordered me, "Don't tell anybody about the patient's death for ten years, for you will be hurting the whole VA's system."

The best satisfaction I got was when King Shorty was told to quit. The dream to be a pharmacy director was now in limbo. He could not refer the VA as a previous acting pharmacy director, for his records were lacking in integrity. He now works in a nearby hospital as a regular registered pharmacist. He could never be a pharmacy director now, for many people knew him and were angry with him and would interfere in his promotions.

Cobra was having difficulty with the new pharmacy director. One time when we were about to have a supervisor's meeting, he asked me to help him. He wanted me to relay to the new director that he was a good man. I answered, "You want me to tell a lie? Even if you implore me, I don't know how to do it, and I know I cannot do it. I could not tell a lie, especially if it concerns you." Cobra later resigned and worked with King Shorty in the same hospital. Both are now registered pharmacists. After six months, he was dismissed. The rumor was that Cobra was dismissed for sexual harassment.

Discrimination was proven, and I became a pharmacist supervisor. Though the VA paid my lawyer, the compensation given was very **minimal**. In this case, the common saying "the victim has no right at all" is partly true. The people who testified for me died, were terminated, or got sick, which caused me much tension, grief, and feelings of guilt, thinking that I was the cause of their pain and early death. I was hit, intimidated, harassed, watched all the time, given more work than other pharmacists, written up for suspension, denied vacations, and screamed at in front of my peers. The hardship, the shame, the harassment, and the violence was such that a normal human being could hardly take it. I was glad, though, for the powerful King Shorty had been forced to resign, even though Cobra stayed for a while. Both have tasted their own medicine. The piranhas are **both** now only licensed pharmacists, working at a local hospital pharmacy. I am hoping they will be forever banned by the VA. The **injustice** is that their pharmacy licenses, including that of Queen Bee, were **not** revoked, especially because Queen Bee had killed a patient.

Chapter 20
Result on the Patient's Death

During the trial, the truths were misrepresented and twisted. On narcotic record evidence, the culprits said that a topographic error had occurred, and the judge believed them. I believe the judge sided with King Shorty's management. All in all, I believe it was a kangaroo court. In Paul's case, if one saw somebody stealing, would they just keep quiet and **not** report it? His testimony was not believed for the reason that he was a whistleblower.

I asked myself, "What will the VA do?" A patient died due to the negligence of a favored employee. Would the VA compensate this patient's s family? I doubted it, for I believed the people in power did not want this incident to ever see the light of day. I also believed that they wanted to protect the culprit, for she was the Chosen One. It was her negligence that resulted in the death of one veteran—a veteran who served this country—and the VA did not care for him the right way.

Was Queen Bee reprimanded or penalized by management or the acting director of pharmacy? Of course not, for she was the favored one. King Shorty told her to **resign** to prevent her from being chastised and losing her pharmacy license.

After this true story, how many veterans will lose their desire to go to the VA? Will it affect the services the VA is providing? Are there other victims? If so, where are their rights? In this case, the victim was a veteran who gave his youth to serve this country, and he was not treated right.

Chapter 21
Result of the Inspector General Investigation

Several times, one staff member from the accounting department came to me fanning a check from the former president of the union, showing them to me. That president of the union was also our former subordinate as a pharmacy technician. He was now paying for the stolen drugs. The VA was able to recuperate the stolen money but caused the death of the whistleblower, Laurence Paul Pinheiro.

This book was **not** written to demean the Veteran's Administrations health care system. The VA system has an **honored cause.** It is an extension of the deserved services provided for the veterans by the country they serve with honor. This book's purpose is to enlighten others to be cautious when they or their loved ones seek the services of the VA, for many use the VA for power, greed, fraud, and control in many aspects. It is my hope that this behavior has been reduced or stopped completely. Also, the fact that our soldiers and veterans are not receiving enough for a decent living is a serious issue. Many veterans are still seeking food in trash bins, for their benefits are not enough. They may need hospitalization or counseling for dependency on drugs, and now their numbers have decreased so dramatically.

Chapter 22
Being a Supervisor

Being a supervisor has lots of privileges. Different jobs open in the nation's VA were forwarded to us, and I relayed these to people who had the talent and incentive for better jobs. Several said that they would love to do the job but were scared they were not capable to do it. I often asked, "Why not?"

The answer was almost always the same with many: "I don't have the experience."

"Yes," I said, "but you have the integrity and talent to be one of the best supervisors." I told each one, "Don't worry, management will train you."

So, many had promotions, and several were relocated to places where they wanted to live when they were promoted. I received many angel figurines and angel pins from subordinates when they left. They left for better employment, but most said that they would continue their education and would try their best to get a profession that would give them a better future. I received lots of thank you letters, many of which said, "Because you inspire me, I have now a better job, and I even teach my children to study hard so they will be better citizens when they grow up."

Two pharmacy technicians became pharmacists, and four became nurses. One earned a degree in finance, and another became a med tech supervisor. These I know for sure. I am sure there were more, for I encouraged many. One time I was in San Francisco for a continuation education class, and I went to the Fisherman's Wharf to see the place after the class. Someone shouted my name, and at the same time, a girl came running toward me. I knew she was once my subordinate, but I had forgotten her name. She was so happy and said, "I have to treat you to dinner, for I just passed the Pharmacy Board exam. Because of your advice and your belief in me, I studied hard, and now I am a pharmacist, just like you. You said I have talent, not to waste it, and to be somebody someday. Now I am somebody." We had a nice dinner and she told me her struggles while in school but said happily, "It was worth it."

For these reasons, I decided to write this book, for it will remind others that veterans deserve to be cared for in an excellent manner, and if wrong has been done, it should be righted and not hushed up. I also believe it will **open the eyes of those concerned,** making known that many are liberally using the VA institution for money and power. Many abuses of different kinds have happened, and I believe they are still happening. **The actions of two vicious people, King Shorty and Cobra, caused the early death of three good, hardworking employees and one very young veteran patient. Joe G. with no fault of his own, had his license revoked. In my opinion, King Shorty, Queen Bee, and Cobra's licenses should have been revoked. Their offenses were very grave.**

Chapter 23

Tips on How to Get the Best Healthcare

You are a veteran! You gave your youth, your strength, and your ambitions to serve this country you love so much. You were wounded, traumatized, and exposed to different chemicals, and you became depressed and affected by many other illnesses during your service.

In return, the people of the United States should give you the best healthcare the world can offer. This nation has given so much to foreign lands, so before them, it should be you. We should take care of you with the best of our ability and our resources, and for you, our care must be **unlimited.**

When health care workers know you are very interested in your health care, each one will be cautious and will do their best **not** to commit mistakes and will be very careful in caring for you.

SUGGESTIONS FOR BETTER CARE

1. Have a record book that you always bring with you to your doctor's visit. One might need it for future reference. Record everything that happened at your visit, including the date, time, and

address of the place you went to have your care. Sometimes you are referred to another facility, where some treatment will be done. Record the address and do everything in recording the treatment.

2. Be sure to record all the names of doctors, nurses, pharmacists, and technicians who took care of you.

3. Have an allergy bracelet made so caretakers will not miss it and mention any allergies at your visit.

4. When you are seen by the doctor, write down the date, time seen, who saw you, and what was said and done to you.

5. What did the doctor tell you about your sickness?

6. Tell him about the sickness that happened, how you feel, and how you got this illness, if you know.

7. Do you need an operation? If the doctor says yes, look for a second opinion.

8. Ask for advice to prevent the sickness from happening again.

9. Above all, eat the recommended foods and take the necessary vitamins stated for you.

10. What are the names of the medicines given to you? Are they liquids, tablets, or capsules, and what color are they? What are they

for, what amount is to be taken, and what is the frequency of time in which the medicine should be taken?

11. Ask the MD what kind of side effects there are, if any, what food to avoid, when to take the medicine, and if you can take it with food or on an empty stomach.

12. Ask the MD if there are possible complications with the drugs you are taking now, if you have any.

13. Ask the doctor if the medicine you are given can affect your kidney or liver.

14. If pregnant or planning to become pregnant, ask the doctor if the drug he is prescribing you affects pregnancy or your baby.

15. Ask the doctor if you can drink alcohol with the drug you are receiving.

16. Record dates for your appointments and the dates you were not able to comply with any appointment. Record the reason why.

17. Record dates of follow-ups and what the attending doctor said.

18. Bring the book with you to all appointments so you can enter pertinent data right away.

19. Were you satisfied in today's visit with your doctor?

20. Did you have any doubts in your doctor's ability or the ability of other people who saw you?

21. How were you treated? If you were treated unkindly in any way, ask for another doctor.

SUGGESTIONS FOR IMPROVING THE VA

1. Encourage whistleblowers and thank them for what the VA was able to collect back from what had been lost. Whistleblowers seem to be the guardians of the VA, and they help prevent the staff from doing corrupt actions in their work, such as stealing or messing up computers on behalf of people they dislike.

2. Supervisors should make an annual report that they did their job impartially and be honest at all times in dealing with drugs.

3. Treat veterans like your equal, not beneath you.

4. Say thank you to every veteran or soldier you encounter.

5. Treat every veteran with respect. You owe your living from them (your job).

6. Due to their sickness or pain, every veteran must receive understanding and compassion when coming in for treatment.

EMPLOYEES:

1. Employees should be allowed to work a second job to a maximum of forty-eight hours a week. Distances from the second job should also be taken into consideration. A very tired person does not have the ability to do his duties efficiently.

2. On-the-job integrity of employees should be included on yearly evaluations.

3. Employees should notify the VA if they have a second job. This prevents an overworked employee who works in the VA from doing an inefficient job. Also, it prevents mistakes.

4. Employees must be strict on working time. Many employees goof around while on duty. Some groups play games in the hospital corridors while on duty.

5. Supervisors must avoid favoritism, which is the main reason subordinates are offended.

6. Supervisors should be mentors to those who have talent and work hard. They will be helping to produce successful people and better citizens.

www.ingramcontent.com/pod-product-compliance
Ingram Content Group UK Ltd.
Pitfield, Milton Keynes, MK11 3LW, UK
UKHW022223230426
12048UKWH00016BA/1032